MW00896566

UNCOMMON WOMEN

writers

Erin Butler

Uncommon Women: Writers

Copyright © 2017
Published by Scobre Educational
Written by Kevin Scarpati

All rights reserved.

Printed in the United States of America.

No part of this book may be reproduced in any manner whatsoever without written permission, except in the case of brief quotations embodied in critical articles and reviews.

Scobre Educational
42982 Osgood Road
Fremont, CA 94539

www.scobre.com
info@scobre.com

Scobre Educational publications may be purchased for educational, business, or sales promotional use.

Cover design by Sara Radka
Layout design by Nikki Ramsay
Edited by Kirsten Rue and Lauren Dupuis-Perez
Copyedited by Malia Green
Images sourced from iStock, Shutterstock, Alamy, and Newscom

ISBN: 978-1-62920-582-3 (hardcover)
ISBN: 978-1-62920-581-6 (eBook)

table of contents

As a young woman, Mary Ann Evans gained access to an important library in England, which later influenced her writing.

Chapter One
GEORGE ELIOT

In the middle of the winter of 1857, a publisher named John Blackwood came to work to find a letter he never would have expected. It came from a potential new writer, and he did not even know the writer's name. The mysterious author wrote bluntly that they would keep their identity a secret by refusing to reveal their real name. Never before had Blackwood seen one of his writers so eager to conceal their identity.

The person who wrote the letter, however, was not like any author Blackwood had published before. In fact, it was the very thing that set this author apart that made them so secretive. Unlike other important authors being published at the time, she was a woman. She disguised herself with the name George Eliot.

DID YOU KNOW?

Though women mainly wrote novels during the 1800s, two of the century's most important poets were women: Elizabeth Barrett Browning and Christina Rossetti.

Though it might seem unbelievable now, women writers in the past had a difficult time getting published and being taken seriously. This was the reality in Victorian times for writers like George Eliot, whose real name was Mary Ann Evans, and the Brontë sisters, Charlotte, Emily, and Anne. These authors are very well known today, and their novels have become classics that people still read all over the world, more than 100 years after their publication. Some of their most popular novels include *Jane Eyre*, *Wuthering Heights*, and *Middlemarch*. Many have been adapted for the screen as movies and miniseries.

However, in their own times, female writers like Evans and the Brontë sisters faced the risk of rejection simply because they were women. Though some women writers were being published at the time, critics and the public rarely considered their books to be serious literature. Instead, they thought that female writers only wrote silly romances, and that it might be "bad manners" to write fiction at all.

There was clearly much more that female writers wanted to say in their novels. They wanted to express political opinions and talk about the way women were treated. In addition, they had new ideas about moving the art of writing into the future. In order to be taken seriously, Evans and the Brontë sisters used male pen-names, or pseudonyms. This meant that readers and critics who picked up their books would think they were reading a man's

NOVELS
OF
GEORGE ELIOT

VOL. II.
MILL ON THE FLOSS
WITH ILLUSTRATIONS

Other authors who have used pen names include Mark Twain, Lewis Carroll, and Dr. Seuss.

work and judge the books based on that standard.

Even today, Mary Ann Evans is better known as George Eliot. Her novels, which are still in print, have the name George Eliot on the cover.

Mary Ann Evans was born on November 22, 1819 in Warwickshire, England. Evans was a bright child and a **voracious** reader. Unlike most girls in this era of the 19th century, she received a good education. She went to a number of different boarding schools and put a lot of effort into her studies. This was, in part, because people considered her plain, and so her family worried she would not get married. She had a great desire for knowledge. Instead of focusing on becoming a wife, Evans dedicated herself to her family and to her studies. While doing so, she discovered a love of learning.

In 1836, Evans's mother died, forcing her to leave school in order to help her father at the family home. Even though she was not technically in school,

Mary Ann Evans changed the spelling of her real name even before she had a pen name. Once, for example, she went by Marian.

learning had become very important to her. She started to teach herself by reading lots of books and writing letters to her old tutor. In this setting, a new Mary Ann Evans was born.

Evans's new life began in 1842. The day after the New Year, she told her father that she would not go to church with him anymore. Her father was shocked. Evans had always been strict about her Christian faith, and in any case, it was expected that she, as a young English woman, would go to church. It would be unladylike not to go. Nevertheless, Evans refused. With all the reading she had been doing, including books about theology—the study of religion—she was starting to question the beliefs she had taken for granted. She no longer thought it was right for her to go to church, and her father threatened to throw her out of the house for her disobedience.

Evans and her father eventually made up, but only after she agreed to go to church again. This did not mean, however, that she was giving up on her new self-discovery. In fact, she was making friends with many free-thinkers and progressive people in England. They had new ideas about social conditions and **morality**. Two of her most important friends were Charles and Cara Bray, who were political and philosophical **radicals**. During this era of new ways of thinking, Evans was right at the forefront. She took every opportunity to learn and to grow, and this included travelling. After her father died in 1849, she went

Evans's childhood home, Griff House, still looks much like it did in the 1800s. The house influenced various settings in her books.

to Europe with some of her intellectual friends, and met even more people with new points of view.

Throughout all of these changes, Evans never forgot her love of reading. Her literary career was slowly but surely starting. In 1846, she published her first book, a **translation** called *The Life of Jesus, Critically Examined*. In the following years, she continued doing translations, but her career became even broader. This began when she met John Chapman, who ran a magazine called *The Westminster Review*. Evans soon began working for him. She became the assistant editor for the magazine, though considering the huge amount of writing, editing, and other work she accomplished, she was more like the editor-in-chief.

DID YOU KNOW?

The *Westminster Review* began in 1824. It aimed to publish radical English viewpoints.

Already, Evans was living a life that was not at all conventional for a woman of her time. She was single and independent, and she held an important job working behind the scenes in the literary world. This was at a time when few women were writing or getting published, and even those lucky few were not taken seriously. Needless to say, it was groundbreaking to have a big job in publishing.

Then came the event that would truly change Evans's life and end any desire to lead the life that was traditionally expected of her. In 1851, she met an intellectual scholar named George Lewes. Evans and Lewes very quickly fell in love and decided to move in with one another. The problem was that Lewes was already married, and he could not divorce his wife. However, from the time they began living together until Lewes died, they considered themselves married. Evans's family and friends disagreed, and they shunned her because of her improper behavior.

George Lewes had many jobs during his life, including biographer, literary critic, dramatist, novelist, philosopher, actor, scientist, and editor.

Around the same time, Evans began to develop confidence in herself as a writer. She had always loved to write, but she had never given serious thought to writing fiction. By now, she had already gained success in her publishing job, and when Lewes told her that she had a real talent and encouraged her, she finally published some stories **anonymously**. This was not enough, however. She had a lot more to say that would not fit into the short length of a story. Yet Evans knew that she was a woman, and women in 19th-century England were only supposed to write romances. There was also the issue of Evans's scandalous reputation, which meant the public might judge her fiction based on her life rather than her writing.

Evans and Lewes came up with the idea to use a pseudonym for her novels. She chose the name George Eliot, which made a reference to her husband's name. Even John Blackwood, the publisher to whom she wrote the letter about her pen name, did not know at first that she was actually a woman. Evans, as George Eliot, enjoyed the freedom of writing about life in England, political thoughts, and the workings of people's minds without being judged either for her gender or for her life.

In 1859, "George Eliot's" first novel, *Adam Bede*, was published. The book became very popular. English readers discussed the novel itself, but they were speculating even more about who this mysterious George Eliot could be. No one guessed that this intelligent, well-written book had been produced by a woman.

When Eliot finally revealed her true identity, her writing had become so well-liked that the public had no choice but to accept her. In fact, they welcomed her into society, and she became a famous and popular writer. By the time she died in 1880, she had published many novels, including her epic, *Middlemarch*, and had broken new ground for all the writers who would come after her.

Adam Bede, illustrated here, is a historical novel by George Eliot, set in 1799.

As children, the Brontës wrote more books than they did as adults.

Chapter Two
THE BRONTË SISTERS

Around the same time that Mary Ann Evans was forging a path of her own, a little family on the moors of Yorkshire, England, was creating its own place in the literary world. The Brontë family had an incredible love for fiction, books, and learning, and it was this shared interest that bound them together. Storytelling became especially important to the children after their mother died, followed by the deaths of the two eldest daughters. The remaining children, Charlotte (born in 1816), Branwell (the only son, born in 1817), Emily (born in 1818), and Anne (born in 1820) lived with their father in the family home, where they were often isolated from other people. As a result, the siblings spent a lot of time with one another and made their home a haven for their stories.

Charlotte, Emily, and Anne Brontë were all active and prolific writers from childhood on. They wrote stories and poems and even created their own fictional worlds together. Charlotte and Branwell created imaginary kingdoms called Glass Town and Angria. They based the world and its events on the

> ### DID YOU KNOW?
> The Brontës' father, Patrick, was originally from Ireland. In contrast to Patrick's love of learning and reading, most of his Irish family could not read.

news they heard about British exploration and other important historical events at that time in England. Their younger sisters, Emily and Anne, joined in, but they later created the kingdom of Gondal to bring their own ideas to life.

All four Brontës made up characters for their worlds and spent much of their time putting them into stories and plays—they even drew maps of the imagined lands. Entire afternoons went by with the children sitting at home with one another and telling stories about the worlds they had created. Most of the stories about Gondal have been lost, but there are diary entries by Emily and Anne that tell us about their creation. Many of the stories by Charlotte and Branwell were bound in tiny books and survived, and can still be read today.

From the very start, the Brontë sisters showed that they were not going to settle for what was expected of them as girls: the fantasy stories that they created

Charlotte Brontë originally wanted to be an artist. She exhibited two of her drawings in 1834.

were inspired by toy soldiers that had been given to their brother. All their early works proved to be important writing lessons for the girls. They experimented with different styles and different voices, and began to think about what it meant to be a writer. Even as they got older, they still wrote about their imaginary kingdoms, making them more and more elaborate.

At this time in England, education was hard to come by for people who were not wealthy—and male—so the sisters exercised their minds by telling stories. However, education was important to the Brontë family, and the girls did get some formal teaching. The schools they attended proved very influential in their lives and became important parts of their fiction. Charlotte summarized her school experience in her novel *Jane Eyre*, with her depiction of Lowood School, the harsh and severe school that Jane Eyre attends. Charlotte's description was a critical one and showed how unhealthy the schools were—a fact that hit close to home, since her older sister had died while away at the school.

The Brontës also read avidly from childhood, and many of the stories they read influenced their early tales of Angria, Glass Town, and Gondal. As young women, all three sisters continued learning when they could, while also taking jobs as teachers and **governesses** to earn money. These jobs also became part of their fiction. Most of what they learned, though, was self-taught from the many books they read.

In 2016, the Northern Ballet celebrated Charlotte Brontë's 200th birthday with a ballet performance of *Jane Eyre*.

By 1846, the sisters had branched out from their tales of fantasy and had begun to write different kinds of literature. That year, they pooled their writing and published a book of poetry. Like Mary Ann Evans, the Brontës were worried that readers and critics might not take their book seriously because they were women. Because of this, they published their book under the names Currer, Ellis, and Acton Bell so that readers would think they were men. The pseudonyms cleverly preserved the girls' initials. Unfortunately, the book of poetry sold very poorly, though critics reviewed it quite positively.

After publishing their first book as a team, the Brontë sisters became confident enough in their abilities to devote themselves more fully to writing. In 1847, Charlotte and Anne both published their first novels. Anne published *Agnes Grey*. Charlotte, still using the name Currer Bell, published *Jane Eyre*, which would become a huge hit. The novel is about a proud and independent orphan, Jane, trying to find her place in the world as an intelligent yet poor woman. This character greatly resembled Charlotte. Jane grows up to become a governess and must experience a journey of trial, heartache, and strength of spirit.

Even though the public loved *Jane Eyre*, critics were not always as kind, especially when they found out that Currer Bell was actually a woman named Charlotte Brontë. The novel and its main character were bold and honest about real life and true feelings, which was a rare thing for anyone to write about at the time, especially women. Female writers were expected to write about morals and lessons, and the stories they were publishing at that time were almost like cookie-cutter reproductions of the same ideas. *Jane Eyre* definitely was not cut from any mold. Many critics even went so far as to call the novel and its author "unwomanly."

In 1848, Anne published her second novel, *The Tenant of Wildfell Hall*, and Emily published her only novel, *Wuthering Heights*. Again, even though the novels were popular, the public was very critical. They judged the books by different standards, since their authors were women.

The Brontës' books have been adapted as films many times. Pictured here is the 1998 version of *Wuthering Heights*.

Sometimes, this meant that critics would call a book immoral or inappropriate when they thought that the Brontës were exploring topics that women should not be writing about. For example, Emily's *Wuthering Heights* included honest declarations of love between its characters. Even though romance was not a new topic for women writers, people felt that the kind of honesty that Emily used went too far. Anne's *The Tenant of Wildfell Hall* similarly talked about some realistic but unfortunate parts of life, such as substance abuse, that were usually ignored in literature.

DID YOU KNOW?

The Brontës still have a large fanbase today. Readers can visit the Brontë Parsonage Museum in England or even join a literary society called the Brontë Society.

Even when critics praised the Brontë sisters' novels, they still used a double standard: since they were women, their writing was judged differently than books by male authors. Critics liked to say that their novels were good for a male writer, but especially good for a female writer. One critic wrote about *Jane Eyre*, for example, "A book more unfeminine, both in its excellences and defects, it would be hard to find in the annals of female authorship." This made the Brontës very upset. They wished that they could be judged simply as writers without having a different judgment system based on their gender. This feeling crept into the letters they wrote and the responses they gave to critics.

As the years passed, the three sisters came back time and time again to their family home as a source of inspiration for their writing. They always encouraged each other to write, and family support was very important to them. As they continued to write novels, the Brontë sisters often did not purposely make statements about the place of women in their society. Instead, they simply wrote honestly and paid attention to the kinds of things other writers ignored. It was

HERE LIE THE REMAINS OF ANNE BRONTE, DAUGHTER OF THE REV. P. BRONTE, Incumbent of Haworth, Yorkshire. She died Aged 28 MAY 28TH 1849

Tuberculosis, also known as consumption, was a common cause of death in the 1800s.

this habit that made them both very popular and regular targets of attack.

By this time, the sisters were publishing under their own names. The public already knew that they were women, and so readers split into two groups. One group loved the novels, while the other criticized them for being shocking and sensational. Unfortunately, the Brontë sisters' writing careers were tragically cut short. Emily and Anne died of **tuberculosis** within months of each other in 1848 and 1849. Charlotte published two more novels and worked hard to preserve her sisters' writings. She even fell in love and got married. However, she also died of tuberculosis in 1855.

After these groundbreaking writers passed away, the public began to look at them differently. This was, in part, due to a biography called *The Life of Charlotte Brontë*, written by another female writer, Elizabeth Gaskell. Even former critics began to respect the work that these literary sisters had created. The Brontës never gave in to the pressure to write what was expected of women. Instead, they wrote about things like challenging love affairs, the experiences of poverty and working life, and what it meant to feel alone. Writers like Gaskell and the general public began to see that the Brontës had given a voice to feelings they had not seen in literature before, which truly changed what it meant to write during the **Victorian era**. Thanks to this realization, the Brontës' novels are considered beloved classics today.

Horses have always been important to S.E. Hinton. Today, she has three of her own.

Chapter Three
S.E. HINTON

The work that writers like Mary Ann Evans and the Brontë sisters did during the Victorian era of the 1800s changed the fate of women writers forever. Finally, people were forced to pay more attention to the books themselves than to whether a writer was male or female. Female writers built on the foundation of the women who came before them, and many of them broke the mold and set new standards over the next hundred years. They claimed a serious spot in the world of books. But even with all these changes, no one was quite prepared for S.E. Hinton.

Susan Hinton was born on July 22, 1948, in the city of Tulsa, Oklahoma. Ever since childhood, Hinton was not

> ### DID YOU KNOW?
> Four of Hinton's books have been made into movies: *The Outsiders; That Was Then, This Is Now; Rumble Fish;* and *Tex.*

satisfied with doing the "girly" things that were expected of her. She loved horses, and she wanted to be a cowboy. This shy and reserved girl also had another love: books. Hinton did not just read books, she wrote them as well. She felt it was her job to write the kinds of books she wanted to read, since she could not seem to find books that satisfied her.

During her childhood, and then as a teenager, Hinton never really fit in with the social groups at her school. But she talked to everyone, and she noticed that there were a lot of similarities between these groups that worked so hard to separate themselves from one another. It was partially this realization that led her to write her first and most famous book, *The Outsiders*.

Hinton wrote *The Outsiders* because, even though she loved reading, she did not like what was available for her to read. As a high school student, all the books she found that were written for young adults were about things like prom dates and the popular girls at school. None of them considered real life or talked about the experiences teenagers actually go through. It was as if the problem of the "silly romance" story from the Victorian age was back again, only this time, it was limited to books for teens.

Hinton wanted to read books that talked about real-life problems and treated teens with respect, rather than assuming they could not handle difficult topics. When she was in her junior year of high school, all her observations about her classmates and about young adult books were coming together when her father became sick with cancer. Suddenly, all the right conditions were in place for her to write *The Outsiders*. She could use her writing to escape the grief she felt for her father, and at the same time, she could produce a story that spoke about her experiences at her high school in Tulsa.

The Outsiders tells the story of three orphaned brothers: Ponyboy, the main

Tulsa, Oklahoma, is in "Green Country," with rolling green hills and woods.

character, and his brothers Darry and Sodapop. Darry takes charge of the family even though he is still very young. The three brothers are members of a gang in town called the Greasers. Their sworn enemies are the Socs, who are rich and live on the other side of town. The book deals with violence between these two gangs in addition to murder, abuse, and other harsh themes that were part of Hinton's real life as a teen in Tulsa. In fact, the death of one of the book's characters mirrors the death of one of her high school classmates. The violence between the Greasers and Socs in her writing found its basis in real rivalries in her school's cliques. One of the main ideas that Hinton tried to get across was that there was really not much of a difference between the Greasers and the Socs deep down, even though they fought constantly. They both had problems and they both truly wanted friendship and happiness.

The Outsiders makes references to many other literary works, especially a poem by Robert Frost called "Nothing Gold Can Stay."

Hinton waited until 1967 to get the book published, two years after she wrote it. She was in college by this time. Teenagers immediately responded to it. There had rarely been a book written just for them that dealt with difficult topics and used their own language. Hinton was the voice of her peers. She knew what they wanted, and she spoke to them.

Critics had mixed reviews. Some of them loved the fact that Hinton was breaking new ground. They applauded her honest and gripping look into the lives of teenagers. Others thought that the book was not well planned or sophisticated enough, or that it was inappropriate for teen readers. One critic wrote, "You can believe a teen-ager wrote it but you can bet teen-agers won't believe what it says"—a judgment that turned out to be very wrong.

Something many teen readers and critics had in common, however, was that they usually assumed Hinton was a man. Instead of listing the author as Susan Hinton, publishers for *The Outsiders* decided to use the name S.E. Hinton. No one could tell just by looking at the name whether S.E. Hinton was male or female. Since the book is written from a male point of view and talks about violence and gangs, most people automatically assumed the writer was male. The publishers did this on purpose. They felt that the "rumbles" and fights would not be believable if readers thought a woman had written them. After the publication of the book, Hinton received letters from fans addressed

In 1983, *The Outsiders* was adapted as an iconic film.

to Mr. Hinton, and critics who met her were always surprised to find out that she was a woman.

DID YOU KNOW?

In the 1960s, writers and filmmakers were beginning to address issues such as gangs and rebellion. Other works during that time include *Rebel Without a Cause* and *West Side Story*.

Hinton had decided early on that she was not going to write the kinds of stories that the public expected of her. She always knew that she wanted to be a writer, and like the other trailblazing female authors who came before her, she did it on her own terms. Thanks to her, writers of young adult books began to realize that they could talk to teens about more than just dates and parties, and that female readers could be just as interested in stories about "tough guys" as male readers. Not only that, but readers and critics alike saw that a writer did not have to be a man to write from a boy's point of view or to talk about topics they thought were only for boys.

Since publishing *The Outsiders*, Hinton has continued to write books, both for young adults and children. They are almost always set in Tulsa, where she still lives, and they often involve references to her love of horses. People are still surprised to learn that Hinton is a shy, private person, considering the kinds of books she writes. It only goes to show that, just as you cannot judge a book by its cover, you cannot judge an author by her book, or a book by its author.

Although Rowling goes by the initials J.K., she does not have a middle name.

HARRY
POTTER
and the Order of the Phoenix

Chapter Four

J.K. ROWLING

In the early 1990s, a young, single mother named Joanne sat in a coffee shop in the United Kingdom, scribbling out a story while her baby daughter slept. She had a college degree, but she was very poor and depended on assistance from the government to survive. She loved to write and was a talented storyteller, but she did not know how much longer she could live without steady employment.

A few years later, Joanne would be one of the wealthiest women in the world, and her story would be the first book in one of the most beloved series in literature. This woman was J.K. Rowling, and her book series would come to be known as the *Harry Potter* series.

J.K. Rowling was born in 1965 in England. Ever since she was a little girl, Rowling knew that she loved to write. In college, she studied the classics so that she could have an even stronger background in writing. After college, she had trouble finding a job, and ended up going to Portugal to teach English. While living in Portugal, she got married and had a daughter. Unfortunately, her marriage fell

DID YOU KNOW?

Many readers remember July 31 as the character Harry Potter's birthday. July 31 is also J.K. Rowling's birthday.

apart, and she came back to the United Kingdom with very little money.

By this time, Rowling had begun to write her first book in the *Harry Potter* series: *Harry Potter and the Sorcerer's Stone*. She focused all her energy on writing when she returned to the United Kingdom and soon finished the book. The next challenge was to get it published, and after six years of writing and more than a year of rejections, one company finally agreed to publish her first novel. There was one condition: her name would have to be listed on the cover as J.K. Rowling instead of Joanne Rowling. The company was afraid that only boys would want to read *Harry Potter*, and that they would not read it if they knew the writer was a woman.

Today, we know that the publishing company did not need to worry. Six *Harry Potter* books followed *Harry Potter and the Sorcerer's Stone*, which tells the story of an orphan boy who discovers he is a wizard with a special

In the United Kingdom, the first Harry Potter book is known as Harry Potter and the Philosopher's Stone.

mission to defeat evil forces in the wizarding world. In addition, companion books and highly successful movies were released. The books are some of the best sellers of all time, with *Harry Potter and the Sorcerer's Stone* alone selling 107 million copies.

The series created its own world of magical spells and potions, and introduced readers to the amazing Hogwarts School of Witchcraft and Wizardry. *Harry Potter* is one of the world's most popular book series, and it has a huge fan base of boys, girls, men, and women of all ages. It is common knowledge now that Rowling is a woman. Previously, it was thought that a fantasy series focusing on magic and told from a boy's point of view had to be written by a man. Rowling has proven that that is absolutely not the case.

Despite their length, some fans begin reading the Harry Potter series at a young age.

DID YOU KNOW?

Throughout history, various women have tried to break into the fantasy genre of writing. One of the most successful was Mary Shelley, the author of *Frankenstein*.

In lots of ways, Rowling has changed young adult literature and fantasy books for the better. Harry Potter builds on a long tradition of fantasy novels and classics going back to ancient times. The unique thing about the series is the way Rowling created distinct, loveable characters and focused on the relationships among those characters. Her new approach brought a love of reading to many new groups of people, young and old alike. Rowling created a new community with her series, one that has made a splash in local book groups and on the internet. Even years after the publication of the final Harry Potter book, fans still communicate with each other, especially online, to talk about the series and its characters. They even write their own spin-off stories, called fan fiction.

Harry Potter has undoubtedly been Rowling's biggest success. She has also written other books for adults, including *The Casual Vacancy* and a crime novel called *The Cuckoo's Calling*. With *The Cuckoo's Calling*, she faced a different problem than before. She knew that her new book would be evaluated based on her reputation for *Harry Potter* and even *The Casual Vacancy*, but *The Cuckoo's Calling* was a new genre for her, and entirely new territory. For this reason, she decided to publish *The Cuckoo's Calling* under the name Robert Galbraith.

When it first came out, the new novel did not sell very many copies. Then,

In total, books in the *Harry Potter* series have sold more than 450 million copies worldwide.

J.K. Rowling illuminates the Empire State Building to mark the USA launch of her non-profit children's organization, Lumos.

the secret of the book's true author was leaked, and it became a hit. Rowling was upset that she had been discovered, but she was also happy to be accepted in a

DID YOU KNOW?

J.K. Rowling wrote three books as companions to *Harry Potter* in support of charities: *Quidditch Through the Ages*, *Fantastic Beasts and Where to Find Them*, and *The Tales of Beedle the Bard*.

new genre. She even plans to keep writing her crime series under the name Robert Galbraith.

Today, Rowling continues to write and publish books. Her hard work and determination to produce *Harry Potter* has given her a truly rags-to-riches story. Now, as one of the wealthiest and most influential women in the United Kingdom, she can focus on charity in addition to her writing. Even among the many awards she has won and all her successes, she never forgets her beginnings and the long road she took to finally be recognized for her creative gifts.

In spite of the strides Rowling has made, her career as a writer makes it clear that women are still not treated with the same respect in the world of books as men writers. Rowling had to face the battle of convincing publishers that *Harry Potter* could be just as successful, if not more so, as fantasy books by male writers. As a result, she chose to leave her gender a mystery until she had achieved success. Ever since, she has been working hard to build the fantasy world for women writers.

Chimamanda Ngozi Adichie's book Americanah was shortlisted for the Baileys Women's Prize for Fiction in 2014. She won the prize for her novel, *Half of a Yellow Sun*, in 2007.

Chapter Five

CHIMAMANDA NGOZI ADICHIE

Today, female writers make up a large portion of published authors. We now live in a world where a writer's work may be thought of as serious and important, regardless of the writer's gender. Female writers are freer than ever to write about any subject they choose, and many popular writers are focusing on the unique experiences of women. They are not afraid to say that they are feminists—people who believe in the equality of genders—and to make this message clear in their storytelling.

One of these writers is Chimamanda Ngozi Adichie, one of the most successful young writers of the present day. Adichie was born in 1977 in Nigeria. She has loved to write for as long as she can remember. It is almost as if she were destined to become a writer: she grew up in the house where Nigeria's most famous writer, Chinua Achebe, had lived.

When she was a child, most of the books Adichie read were about people in the United States or Europe. She did not even realize that a person who lived in Nigeria or who looked like her could be the main character in a story, and so even her own stories were about people who lived lives very different from her own. Then, when she was 10 years old, she read a book called *Things*

Fall Apart by Achebe. The book was different from anything she had ever read. Its main characters were Nigerians, and it dealt with issues that were actually meaningful to her. For the first time, Adichie realized that she not only could—but should—write about the different experiences that other books ignored. The lives of Nigerian people became the focus of her writing.

While still writing, Adichie attended college, first in Nigeria, and then in the United States. She studied medicine in Nigeria, and switched to communication and **political science** in the United States. Then she got a master's degree in creative writing. By this time, she had written quite a bit, including short stories, poems, and a play. She was ready to release her first novel, *Purple Hibiscus*, in 2003. Finally, she could bring stories about Nigeria to Nigerians themselves, and to the whole world. Writing in English meant that she could have a wide audience. There are many languages spoken in Nigeria, but most Nigerians also speak English, and so Adichie's books would be read all over the country.

Adichie has always called herself a feminist, and so strong female characters have been important in her writing. She does not go out of her way to invent characters whose only focus is equality for women. Instead, she represents lots of different women as they really are, and lets their strengths speak for themselves. She is fearless in writing honestly about what women experience, even if that means diving into details about trauma. In her novel *Half of a Yellow Sun*, for example, the main female character has to deal with constant violence and the deaths of many of her family members, and yet she faces these issues with great courage.

DID YOU KNOW?

Many Nigerian writers face challenges in their home country because there are few publishers. However, as writers publish in other countries, Nigerians are steadily reading more and more about their own experiences.

Adichie does not limit her stories to only female characters. She writes about characters of all ages, both men and women. She also often focuses on the Biafran War, a **civil war** in Nigeria in the 1960s that was fought when the Igbo people wanted to **secede** from Nigeria. Many people in places like the United States and Europe do not even know that the Biafran War happened. Although Adichie, who is Igbo, was not yet born when the war was fought, it had a huge effect on her family and community, and so it is important to her writing. Like other female writers, Adichie is not afraid to tackle difficult issues like war and tragedy.

Since publishing her first novel, Adichie has published three more books: *Half of a Yellow Sun*, *The Thing around Your Neck*, and *Americanah*. She has also given lectures to discuss issues like feminism and storytelling. In one of these lectures, she talked about why it was so important for her to write about diverse experiences. She told the audience, "The single story creates stereotypes, and the problem with stereotypes is not that they are untrue, but that they are incomplete. They make one story become the only story." Adichie wants to tell many different stories instead of one incomplete story. Today, she still writes while going back and forth between Nigeria and the United States. She continues to pave the way for women writers all over the world.

Adichie is not alone in continuing the tradition of women writers. Many other women work hard not only to be good storytellers, but also to make sure that female writers are being treated equally and that no voices are left unheard. This is no easy job.

Caitlin Moran's first novel, *How to Build a Girl*, was published in 2014.

One of these writers is Caitlin Moran. She began writing as a teenager and has recently published new novels for adults. Her books, including *How To Build A Girl* and *How To Be A Woman*, speak honestly about what women's lives are like in today's world. Moran has never been conventional, and her books have not been, either.

Another important female voice in today's literary world is Amy Tan. Though she did not begin writing until she was an adult, Tan has become a very successful author. Her most popular book is *The Joy Luck Club*. Tan writes about the experiences of women and Chinese Americans, joining the tradition of women writers who want their own unique truths to be heard. Many of her stories are based on her own life or the lives of her family members.

Amy Tan published her first book, *The Joy Luck Club*, in 1989.

For those of us who read in English, writers like Adichie, Moran, and Tan remind us that there are many stories that we have not yet heard, including some of our own. There are cultures, groups of people, lifestyles, and experiences about which we know very little. Perhaps we do not even know they exist. The strong women writers of the present are taking up the job of telling the stories of these people. They show us that women have not always had it easy as authors, but thanks to the work of some uncommon women, they have come a long way. Now, by writing persistently and fearlessly about any and all subjects, they are opening up the literary world to make sure that all groups of people have that same opportunity.

GLOSSARY

anonymously: to be unnamed or unknown

civil war: a war between people of the same country

governesses: women employed to teach children in their home

morality: values about the difference between right and wrong

political science: the study of government and politics

radicals: people who want to completely change some part of society

secede: to withdraw or break away from

translation: the process of turning words or texts from one language into another

tuberculosis: a bad and often deadly disease of the lungs

Victorian era: an era of British history when Queen Victoria ruled (1837-1901) and the British Empire was the most powerful nation in the world

voracious: eagerly and enthusiastically consuming something, such as food or knowledge

BIBLIOGRAPHY

Uglow, Jennifer. George Eliot. New York: Pantheon Books, 1987.

Bodenheimer, Rosemarie. The Real Life of Mary Ann Evans. Ithaca: Cornell University Press, 1994.

"George Eliot." Hutchinson's Biography Database (2011): 1.Supplemental Index. Web. 23 Oct. 2014.

Cohen, Paula Marantz. "Why Read George Eliot? Her Novels Are Just Modern Enough – And Just Old-Fashioned Enough, Too." American Scholar 75.2 (2006): 129-132. Academic Search Complete. Web. 23 Oct. 2014.

Frome, Susan. "The sage of unbelief: George Eliot and unorthodox choices." The Humanist 2006: 27. Academic OneFile. Web. 23 Oct 2014.

Hufel, Alice L. "A hundred conflicting shades: the divided passions of George Eliot." Biblio Nov. 1998: 20+. Academic OneFile. Web. 24 Oct. 2014.

georgeeliot.org/about-george-eliot/the-coventry-years.aspx

i09.com/5800925/the-bronte-sisters-invented-imaginary-realms-and-created-the-first-fan-fiction

bbc.co.uk/history/historic_figures/bronte_sisters.html

Ewbank, Inga-Stina. Their Proper Sphere. Cambridge: Harvard University Press, 1966.

Brontë, Charlotte, Emily Brontë, and Anne Brontë. Introduction. Tales of Glass Town, Angria, and Gondal: Selected Writings. Ed. Christine Alexander. Oxford: Oxford UP: 2010. xiii-xliii. Print.

shinton.com/bio.html#

Daly, Jay. Presenting S.E. Hinton. Boston: Twayne Publishers, 1989.

jkrowling.com/en_US/#/about-jk-rowling/biography

"Rowling, J.K." Encyclopædia Britannica (2014): Research Starters. Web. 9 Nov. 2014.

telegraph.co.uk/culture/books/3666215/From-the-dole-to-Hollywood.html

pennlive.com/entertainment/index.ssf/2013/07/jk_rowling_is_robert_galbraith.html

huffingtonpost.com/2013/07/24/jk-rowling-pen-name-robert-galbraith_n_3644567.html

bustle.com/articles/15839-what-jk-rowling-using-a-male-pseudonym-says-about-sexism-in-publishing

Eccleshare, Julia (2002). "The Publishing of a Phenomenon." A Guide to the Harry Potter Novels. Continuum International. 7.

entertainment.howstuffworks.com/arts/literature/21-best-sellers.htm#page=5

ted.com/speakers/chimamanda_ngozi_adichie

chimamanda.com/about-chimamanda/

l3.ulg.ac.be/adichie/cnaintro.html

l3.ulg.ac.be/adichie/cnabio.html

caitlinmoran.co.uk/index.php/caitlin-moran/

caitlinmoran.co.uk/index.php/category/books/

amytan.net/bio-1.html